Easy Coloring Book For Adults

This Beautiful Relaxing Coloring book belongs to:

Copyright © 2019 Adult Coloring Books

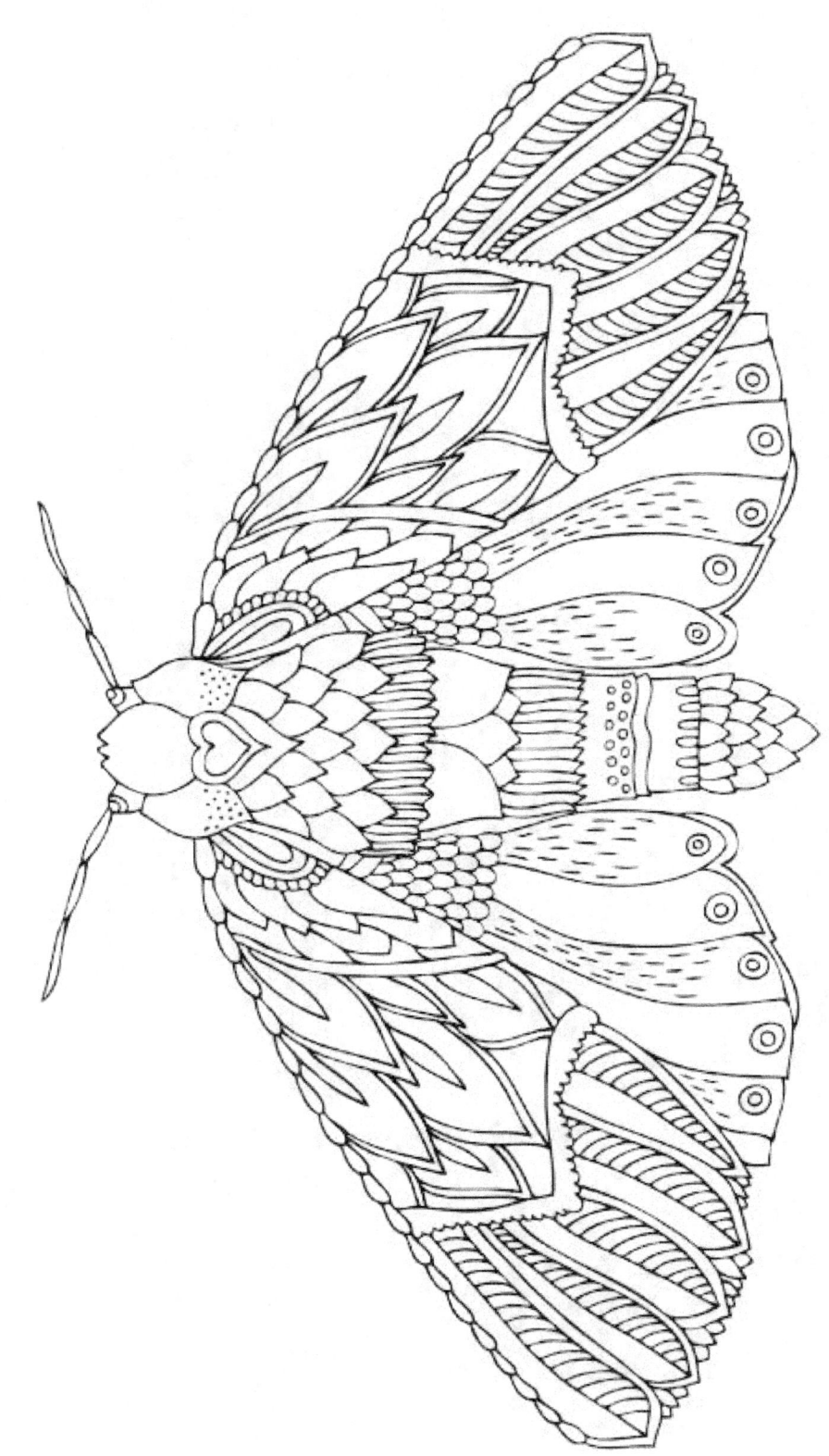

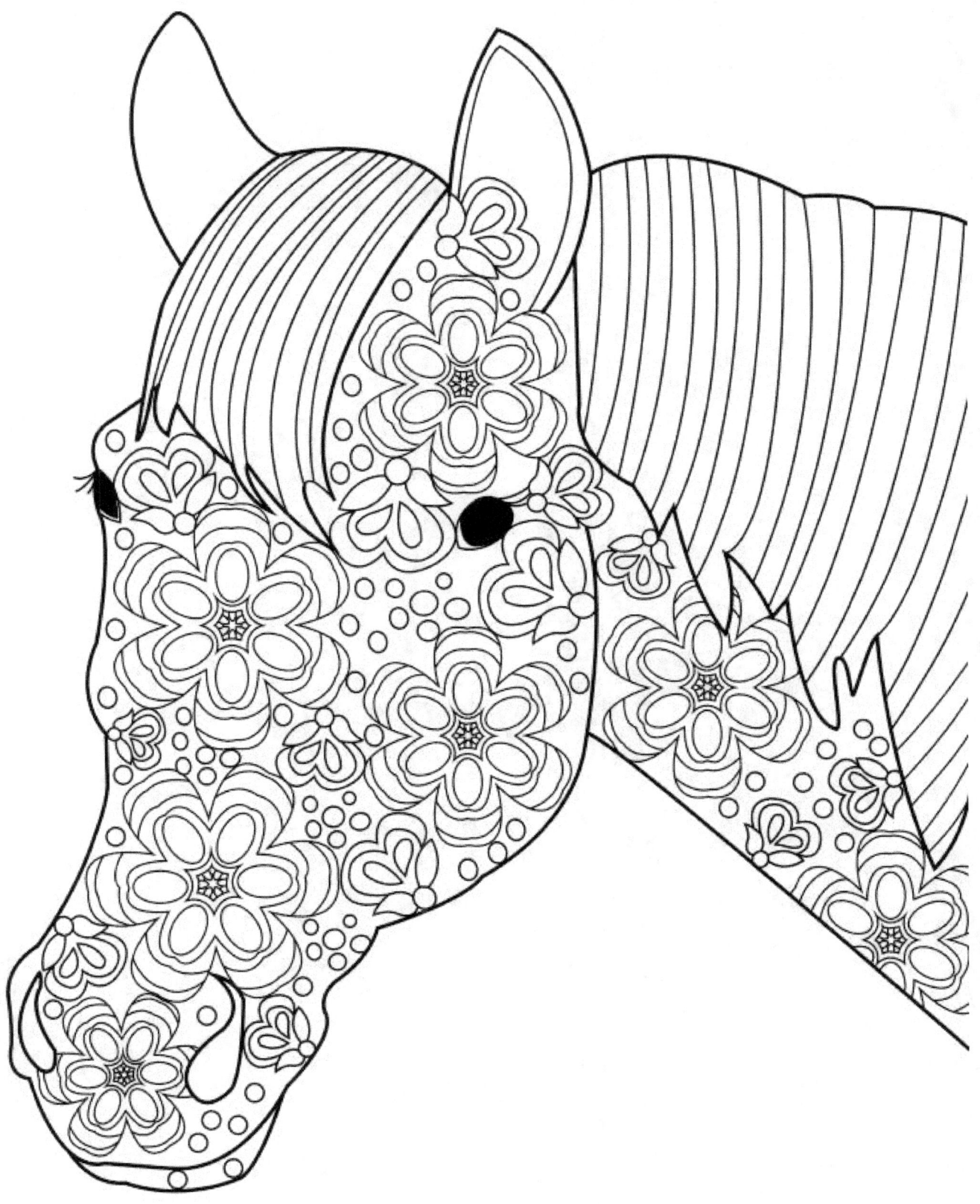

www.ingramcontent.com/pod-product-compliance
Lightning Source LLC
Chambersburg PA
CBHW081011170526
45158CB00010B/3005